"*Water of Life*" is a brilliant representation of the mee which took place, at a well one day, between Jesus a Samaritan woman. This powerful story, of the way som life was completely changed as a result of talking to J can be found in John's Gospel, chapter 4.

The woman in question came from a city called Sychar (Shechem, in the Old Testament), roughly in the middle of Palestine (modern Israel). Samaritan people are half-Jewish and half-Gentile; and, at the time of Jesus, they did not get on well with the Jews. So it was all the more surprising that this person - and a woman at that - even spoke to Jesus, and he to her; quite apart from being influenced by him as deeply as she was.

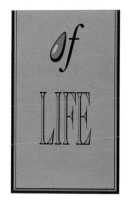

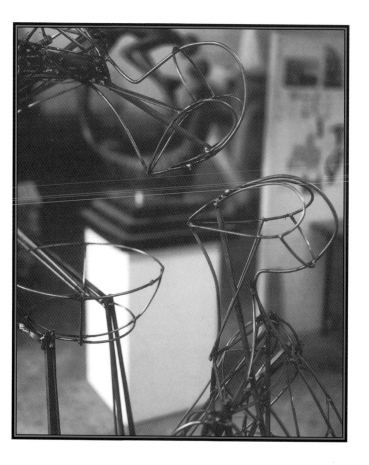

A SKELETON OF STEEL
RODS, BENT AND
WELDED, FORM A RIGID
STRUCTURE ON TO
WHICH THE MODELLING
IN PLASTER BEGINS.

WATER *of* LIFE

Tradition has it that the woman was called Photina (meaning "radiant"); although John tells us little about her background, and does not mention her name at all. But, as the woman's story unfolds, we can learn a good deal about her character.

Evidently the woman was not particularly affluent; otherwise she would not have had to draw water at this well in the first place. On the other hand, she was presumably very beautiful. Whatever her reasons for marrying and divorcing five husbands, and living now with a man to whom she was not married, attractiveness and passion must have played some part in the process!

THE ARTIST
SHAPING THE PLASTER
WITH FILES
AND CHISELS.

So that day the woman came to draw water from the well, which was situated just outside the walls of Sychar. She came at noon: the hottest time of the day. Normally, water would be drawn in the cool of the early morning, or during the evening; so a crisis must have caused her to venture out at midday. But, as she drew close to Jacob's well, she saw a man sitting beside it, looking intently at her. She had no idea who it was. Possibly she wanted to avoid contact with him: both to safeguard her already bad reputation for consorting with men, and so that she could return as soon as possible to her domestic duties at home.

WATER
of
LIFE

THE PLASTER
MODEL SUPPORTED
WITH CHAINS
AND STRAPS.

WATER *of* LIFE

However, as she hauled up the bucket full of fresh water, the man spoke to her. Not surprisingly, given the heat of the midday sun, he asked her for a drink. She must have recognised a Galilean lilt in his voice, because she immediately identified him as Jewish. "How come," she said, "that you, a Jew, ask a Samaritan woman for a drink?" Jews and Samaritans, remember, did not share anything in common.

A SAD AND
DIFFICULT TASK,
WHEN THE FINISHED
PLASTER IS CUT
INTO SECTIONS AND
TRANSPORTED TO
THE FOUNDRY.

She was sizing him up as she spoke, and Jesus was probably holding her with his eyes. When at last he replied, the words were strange: "If you knew the gift of God, and who it is that is saying to you, 'give me a drink,' you would have asked him, and he would have given you living water." The woman was floundering now; for Jesus seemed to be saying that she should be asking him for water, not the other way round. And not just ordinary water, but "living water." What could that possibly mean?

THE CASTING PROCESS. FROM THE VARIOUS SECTIONS OF THE SCULPTURE ARE MADE RUBBER MOULDS, INTO WHICH HOT WAX IS POURED. WHEN THIS SOLIDIFIES, EACH SECTION IS CASED IN A TYPE OF PLASTER. THE WAX IS THEN MELTED, AND MOLTEN BRONZE POURED IN ITS PLACE.

WATER *of* LIFE

But the woman was enjoying the conversation by now, and she wanted to continue it. The crisis in the house would have to wait. Was there a slight mockery in her voice, then, as she went on: "Sir, you have no bucket, and the well is deep. Where do you get that living water?" She had taken him literally. But now Jesus moved the discussion to another level: "Everyone who drinks of this water will be thirsty again, but those who drink the water that I will give them will never be thirsty. The water that I will give will become in them a spring of water, welling up to eternal life."

Still she did not understand. Was this man really promising to liberate her from the unending and tough burden of carrying water from the well back to the house, every morning and evening? Whatever it was, Jesus seemed to be offering at least this freedom, if not a greater one. Desperately, almost, she responded: "Sir, give me this water!"

THE BRONZE
SECTIONS LIE STREWN
LIKE PIECES OF A
JIG-SAW. THEY WAIT
TO BE WELDED BACK
TOGETHER.

At that point no water was produced. Instead, Jesus changed tack. He asked the woman to call her husband, and return to the well! Was he expecting her to need a chaperon? Had the relationship suddenly become so intense? Anyway, she refused to go along with the request; and grudgingly the admission came that she had no husband. The reply this time arrived like a bolt from the blue. "You are right in saying, 'I have no husband'; for you have had five husbands, and the one you have now is not your husband. What you have said is true!"

WATER *of* LIFE

COMING OUT OF THE FOUNDRY AND INTO THE OPEN FOR THE FIRST TIME, THE WORK OF ART IS READY TO BE DELIVERED TO THE CATHEDRAL.

WATER
of
LIFE

This was becoming impossible! How could the conversation continue, if Jesus kept producing trump cards? The woman, frustrated, was probably about to go back home; but something kept her, as she looked into his face again, and saw there neither pity nor judgment, but respect. This time she sidestepped. "I see you are a prophet." Was there a touch of sarcasm in her voice? If so, she tried to cover it up; and quickly she produced instead a reference to the long-standing battle between Samaritans and Jews about the way to worship: "Our ancestors worshipped on this mountain (Gerizim, on the slopes of which they were talking), but you say that the place where people must worship is in Jerusalem."

THE FOUNDRY
CAT HAS ONE LAST
INSPECTION!

Yet again Jesus seized the advantage. He wouldn't let her
go; but nor would he allow her to win the argument.
"Woman," he said, "believe me, the hour is coming when you
will worship the Father neither on this mountain nor in
Jerusalem." Once more, Jesus had lifted the level of
discussion. But then it seemed to slip backwards, and to
suggest a mood of arrogance: "You worship what you
do not know; we worship what we know, for salvation is
from the Jews."

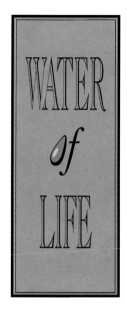

ALL HANDS TO THE
DECK, AS FINALLY THE
SCULPTURE IS READY FOR
THE CRANE TO PICK IT UP
IN ABBEY SQUARE, AND
SKILLFULLY LIFT IT OVER
THE CATHEDRAL
INTO THE ENCLOSED
CLOISTER GARTH.

THE BRONZE BASE
IS FIRST LOWERED
INTO POSITION, AND
THEN BOLTED TO A
STAINLESS STEEL
PLINTH.

WATER of LIFE

The woman was about to pick up that claim as unjustified, when something - about Jesus himself, or about the way he spoke next - stopped her. "The hour is coming, and it is now here, when the true worshippers will worship the Father in spirit and truth." "That's right," she thought; " if we are to honour God, who is the Spirit, we must worship him spiritually and truthfully." God cannot be tied down to a time or a place; he is greater than any temple or church.

AS THOUGH FROM HEAVEN, THE SCULPTURE DESCENDS TO THE POOL. IT IS CAREFULLY POSITIONED, AND THE BOLTS TIGHTENED.

The light had begun to dawn. All that the woman could think to say now was, "I know that Messiah is coming." In reply, the man said, "I am." She was speechless. Had she heard correctly? That was the name by which God had identified himself to Moses on Mount Horeb. So this meant that his Messiah, God's Son, was now sitting on another mountain, talking to a woman about true worship and living water! Jesus said to her, "I am he, the one who is speaking to you." The revelation was complete.

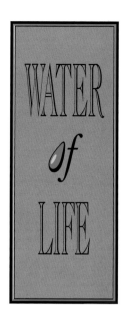

WATER
of
LIFE

FINAL ADJUSTMENTS ARE MADE, WITH THE DEAN, THE ARTIST AND HIS SON WATCHING WITH CONCERN IN THE BACKGROUND.

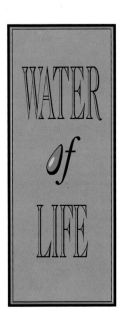

WATER of LIFE

Suddenly, the scene became crowded with people, and alive with activity. The disciples had returned with a picnic, surprised to find Jesus talking with a Samaritan who was also a woman, and unaware that Jesus needed neither food nor drink. "I have food to eat that you do not know about." On the other hand, the woman rushed off to tell others what she had discovered. She left her pot of fresh water at the well, and eagerly shared with her friends in the city the good news that in Jesus the Christ there is to be found a spring of water, welling up to eternal life.

THE ARTIST
APPLYING HEAT AND
ACID TO ACHIEVE
THE DESIRED PATINA.
IT IS THEN SEALED
WITH WAX.